SHARKS

This edition produced
in **1993** for
Shooting Star Press Inc
230 Fifth Avenue
New York, NY 10001

Design David West
Children's Book Design
Illustrations Tessa Barwick, Louise Nevett
Picture Research Cecilia Weston-Baker
Editor Kate Petty

© Aladdin Books Ltd 1987

Created and produced by
Aladdin Books Ltd
28 Percy Street
London W1P 9FF

*First published in the
United States in 1987 by*
Gloucester Press

ISBN 1-56924-004-3

Printed in Belgium

This book tells you about sharks — how they live, what they look like and how they survive in the ocean today. Find out some surprising facts in the boxes on each page. The Identification Chart at the back will help you when you see sharks in zoos or aquariums.

or

The little square shows you the size of the shark. Each side represents about ten feet (3m).

A red square means that a shark is being studied by scientists. Turn to the Survival File.

The picture opposite is a White-tip Shark photographed in the Red Sea

SHARKS

Alwyne Wheeler

SHOOTING STAR PRESS

Introduction

There were plenty of sharks in the sea 350 million years ago, long before mammals, birds or other fish were common. So sharks are survivors of the prehistoric age, ideally suited to the world they live in. There are about 340 different kinds of shark known today. Many of them are magnificent creatures.

Like all other animals, sharks need to be protected — perhaps more so, because so few people like them. In fact, most sharks live far out at sea and are unlikely to attack a human.

Scientists are trying to find out more about sharks. Swimmers may be able to avoid shark attacks if they understand why sharks behave in certain ways.

Contents

◁ **Close encounter with a Blue Shark**

Streamlined for speed

Sharks are perfectly built for life in the sea. Their streamlined shape and the way in which the high tail fin is balanced by the pectoral fins means that they can swim and dive effortlessly. Their long tails drive them along at a gentle cruising speed. When hunting they can travel at about 22mph (35kph) to catch fast-swimming animals such as squids, anchovies and flying fish.

Many sharks, like the Blue Shark, are powerful long-distance swimmers too. Blue Sharks are found all around the world where the sea is warm. In summertime they follow the warmer water. Blue Sharks live near the surface. The clear blue of their backs and pure white coloring of the underside are typical of sharks that live near the surface of the sea.

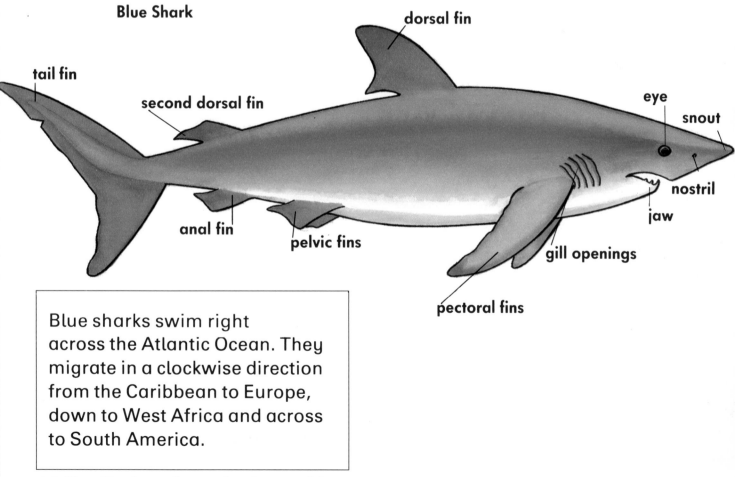

Blue Shark

dorsal fin

tail fin

second dorsal fin

eye

snout

nostril

jaw

anal fin

pelvic fins

gill openings

pectoral fins

Blue sharks swim right across the Atlantic Ocean. They migrate in a clockwise direction from the Caribbean to Europe, down to West Africa and across to South America.

◁ **A Blue Shark, perfect swimming machine**

Non-stop swimmers

Active sharks, like the White-tip Shark, live near the surface of the sea and keep moving all their lives. They never stop swimming to go to sleep. Sharks that live on the seabed may lie still for hours on end. Some may find underwater caves in which they can snooze. Unlike most fish, sharks do not have an air bladder to help them float. Instead they have a large oily liver which does the same job.

Sharks get a constant supply of oxygen when they swim continuously. A steady stream of water flows over their gills and out of the five gill slits on each side of the head. The gills extract oxygen from the water. If the shark stops swimming or is trapped, the water no longer flows over its gills. Then it cannot take in oxygen and it drowns.

White-tip Shark

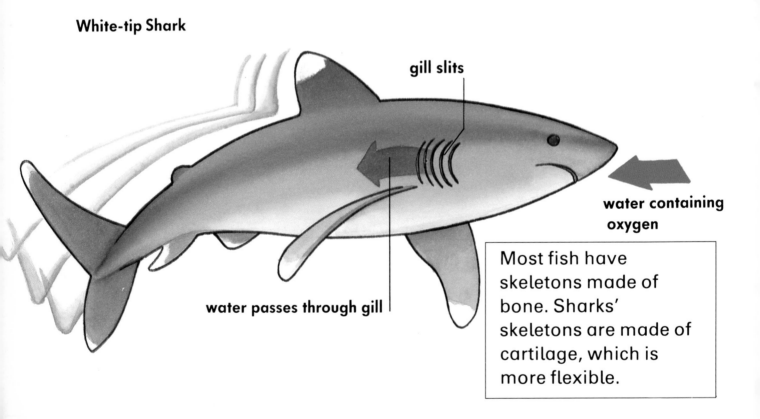

gill slits

water containing oxygen

water passes through gill

Most fish have skeletons made of bone. Sharks' skeletons are made of cartilage, which is more flexible.

The White-tip Shark is probably the most common of the big sharks in the open sea ▷

Extra senses

Sharks depend very heavily on smell to find their food. Their nostrils are quite large and far apart. When searching for food, sharks swing their heads from side to side and turn where they smell the strongest scent. Scientists think that sharks sometimes bump an object to "taste" it through taste cells in the skin. Incredibly sensitive cells on a shark's snout pick up the tiniest electrical discharges from a nearby animal. They can also feel vibrations along the sensitive "lateral line" when an animal is struggling in the water. On top of all this, they can smell blood in the water even when it is diluted ten million times. So they do not depend on their eyesight to hunt their prey.

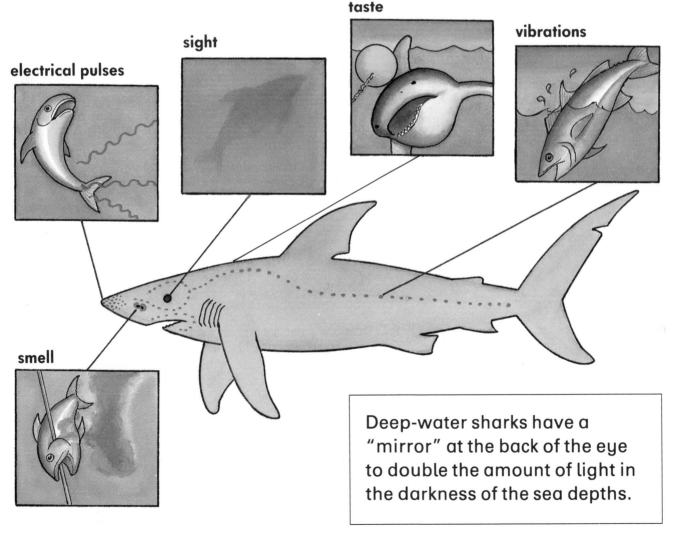

electrical pulses

sight

taste

vibrations

smell

Deep-water sharks have a "mirror" at the back of the eye to double the amount of light in the darkness of the sea depths.

◁ **A Lemon Shark**

Teeth for biting

Sharks never stop growing new teeth. All of them have many rows of teeth in both jaws. As the front ones wear down and fall out they are replaced by new teeth from inside the jaw. The Lemon Shark replaces about 30 teeth each week.

The shape of a shark's teeth depends on the food it eats. The Tiger Shark often eats turtles. It has saw-edged teeth in both jaws. It bites the turtle and then shakes its head slowly from side to side so that the teeth saw through the shell and bones. The Port Jackson Shark has large, flat teeth for crushing sea urchins, prawns and crabs. The Nurse Shark uses its heavy jaws for crushing shellfish while its hundreds of small, pointed teeth hold the food still.

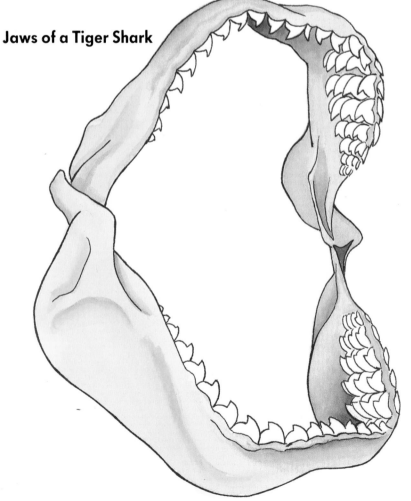

Jaws of a Tiger Shark

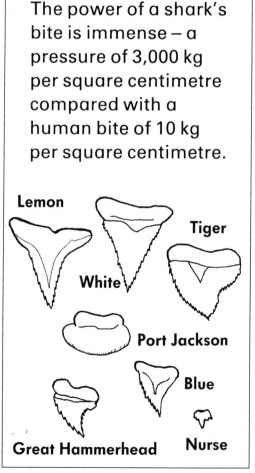

The power of a shark's bite is immense — a pressure of 3,000 kg per square centimetre compared with a human bite of 10 kg per square centimetre.

Lemon

Tiger

White

Port Jackson

Blue

Great Hammerhead

Nurse

A Sand Tiger Shark showing its teeth ▷

Garbage collector

Most active sharks have sharp-edged or spiky teeth. They feed on many different kinds of prey. Some, like the Blue Shark, eat fast-swimming squids and all kinds of fish that live in the surface waters. Other sharks, like the Tiger Shark, seem to eat almost anything they come across – dolphins, sea mammals, sea birds and turtles. Fishermen have found old boots, tin cans, beef bones, floats from fishing nets, the head of a sheep and even a dead dog inside Tiger Sharks. Much of this was rubbish dumped in the sea. It is easy to see why the Tiger Shark has been called the garbage collector of the sea!

When several sharks pick up the scent of blood they rush in to bite at the prey in a "feeding frenzy."

What a Tiger Shark might eat

other sharks

seabirds

garbage

fish

dolphins

sea mammals

turtles

Once a shark swallowed some identity papers thrown overboard by the captain of an enemy ship who didn't want anyone to find out who he was. His true identity was revealed by a fisherman who discovered the papers inside the shark.

◁ **A striped Tiger Shark**

Fellow travelers

Sometimes sharks travel in groups but often they hunt alone. Even those lone hunters are usually accompanied by smaller fish that swim close by. Pilot fish have dark stripes across their bodies. They hide in the shadow of the shark, protected from their enemies but able to dart out and snap up any suitable food.

Shark suckers and remoras are sucker fish which actually hitch a ride on the shark. They cling to its rough skin by a sucker on top of the head and back. They usually stay close to the shark, feeding on any parasites that attach themselves to it. They also feed on small creatures passing by.

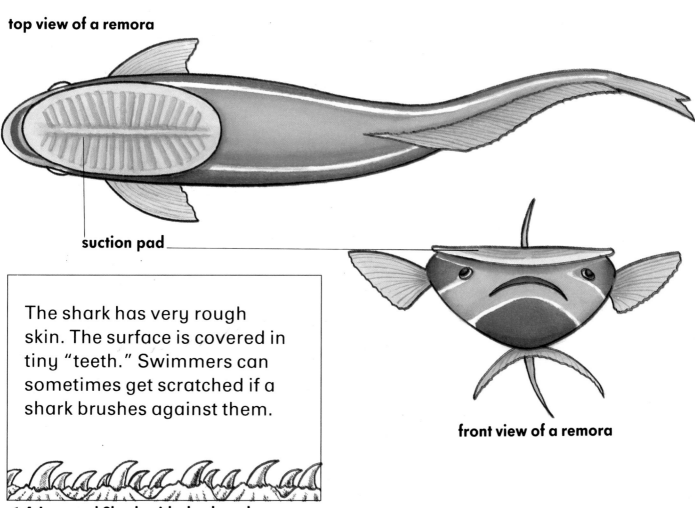

top view of a remora

suction pad

The shark has very rough skin. The surface is covered in tiny "teeth." Swimmers can sometimes get scratched if a shark brushes against them.

front view of a remora

◁ **A Leopard Shark with shark suckers**

Gentle giants

Three kinds of very large shark are harmless, slow-moving giants. The Whale Shark, the biggest known shark at 45 feet (13.7m) long, lives in tropical seas. It swims along sucking in minute animal plankton. Sometimes it feeds on anchovies, sardines and other small fish.

Basking Sharks live in cooler, temperate seas and grow up to about 30 feet (10m). They feed on animal plankton by swimming along with their mouths open.

Megamouth has only been found twice. It grows to 15 feet (4.5m). It lives in deep water and feeds only on deep-sea shrimps. They are attracted by light organs that glow inside its huge mouth.

▽ **A Basking Shark with its mouth open**

◁ **A Whale Shark**

Unsafe waters

Sometimes swimmers are killed by sharks. Altogether there are around 100 shark attacks on people each year, and only about 25 to 30 of the victims die. Almost all attacks take place in the warm waters around the coasts of Australia, South Africa and the warmer coasts of North America. This is partly because the heat seems to make the sharks more aggressive.

Only about 20 kinds of sharks are dangerous. The most dangerous of all is probably the Great White Shark. It grows to at least 21 feet (6.4m), large enough to eat seals, sealions, porpoises and big fish as well as occasional swimmers. Most sharks attack when they are frightened or threatened by a swimmer's approach rather than because they are hungry.

Sharks are attracted by splashing and struggling. If a shark is near by, a swimmer should swim away strongly and steadily and try not to panic.

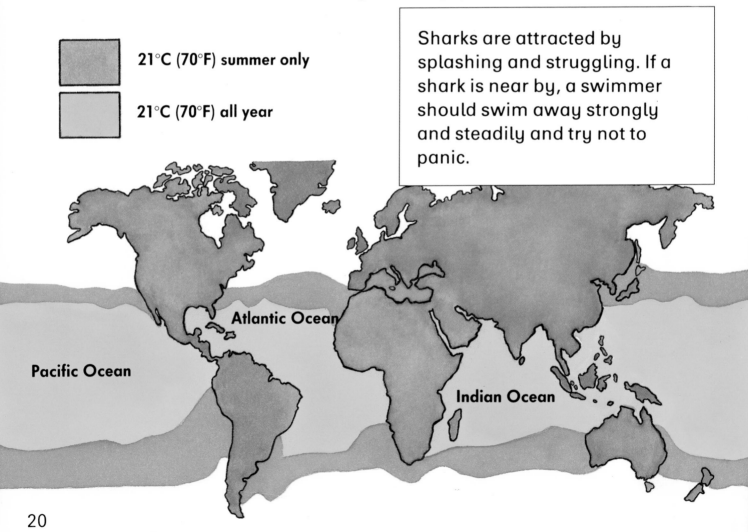

21°C (70°F) summer only

21°C (70°F) all year

Pacific Ocean

Atlantic Ocean

Indian Ocean

Strange sharks

Hammerhead Sharks have flat heads that extend sideways to form a hammer shape. They have an enormous advantage over other sharks. The eyes at the extreme ends of the hammer are able to see all around the shark and their widely spaced nostrils help them smell food at a great distance. Hammerheads are usually the first sharks to arrive at a bait.

The Wobbegong lives on the coasts of northern Australia and Papua New Guinea, usually close to coral reefs. Its mottled coloring and long fringed beard around its head help it to hide among seaweeds and coral. It lies in wait for fishes, crabs, lobsters or octopuses to come close enough to catch.

▽ **A Wobbegong Shark lying near the seabed**

◁ **The strange Hammerhead Shark**

Shark babies

Most fish lay their eggs in the water, but sharks do not just abandon their eggs. Many shark babies are kept inside the mother's body until they are big enough to swim and feed on their own. The Blue Shark sometimes has as many as 50 babies at a time, but others, like the Porbeagle, have only one or two. A Spiny Dogfish carries her 20 babies inside her for nearly two years before they are born.

The Cat Shark lays its eggs in small leathery cases which have long threads at the corners to tangle in seaweed. This stops them being washed away. The baby Cat Shark hatches out after many months when it is about four inches (10cm) long.

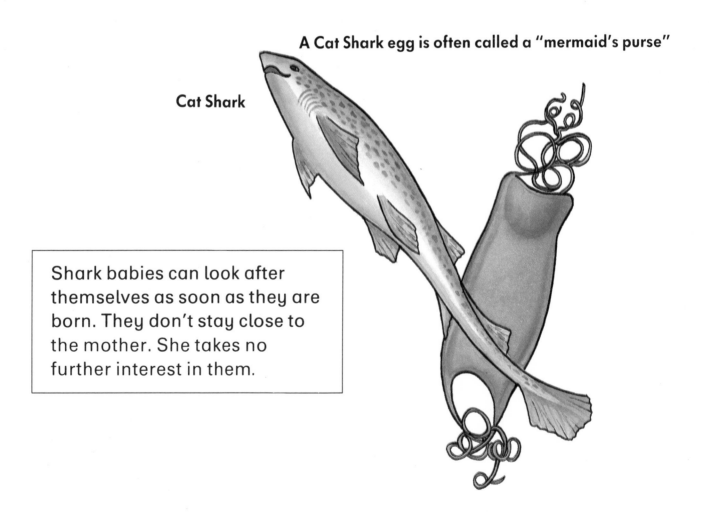

A Cat Shark egg is often called a "mermaid's purse"

Cat Shark

Shark babies can look after themselves as soon as they are born. They don't stay close to the mother. She takes no further interest in them.

A young Port Jackson Shark ▷

Sharks' enemies

Because many sharks are large and can swim quickly there are very few animals that attack them. Some small or newborn sharks are eaten by bigger sharks, and some are attacked by Orca Whales, Sperm Whales and large fish. Dolphins will band together to attack a shark in order to protect their own young. Swordfish have also been known to stab at sharks.

The biggest enemies of sharks are humans. About 30 people a year are killed by sharks, but about 4.5 million sharks are killed by people. In some countries sharks like the Cat Shark and the Spiny Dogfish are used for food.

Dolphins sometimes attack sharks

Some kinds of sharks have been sold for food and appear on restaurant menus.

Survival file

Sharks have survived for millions of years. But even though their ocean habitat is not in any particular danger, they are at risk from the activities of humans who see them as an evil menace. Luckily, there are scientists who want to study sharks and find out more about them. The best place to watch sharks is in their natural surroundings. Divers sometimes stay inside a cage so they cannot be attacked. Then they can safely film the sharks at close quarters. They attract the sharks with a bait of fresh fish.

Filming a Great White Shark from a cage

Experienced divers sometimes swim freely among the sharks. They carry a stick with an explosive head on it to keep the dangerous sharks away. They try to understand the sharks' body language. The way a shark moves when it is swimming toward a diver may tell us whether it is aggressive, frightened, curious, hungry or even playful. Divers "tag" sharks by fastening a number on to a fin. If one is recaptured they can see how it has grown and how far it has traveled.

Diver alongside a Whale Shark

Valerie Taylor testing her shark-suit

Scientists can also learn from sharks kept in captivity. They are studying how they hear, how well they can see, and how much they depend on their sense of smell. They want to find out how the organs that detect faint electric discharges from other animals work. It is important to learn about their sense of taste. If scientists can find a substance that sharks do not like, then swimmers and divers will be able to carry it with them in case of attack.

Ron and Valerie Taylor are Australian naturalists who find sharks so fascinating that they have made them a lifetime's study.

Identification chart

This chart shows you some of the more common sharks. They are drawn to scale to show their comparative sizes. The sides of each square of the grid represent one foot (30cm).

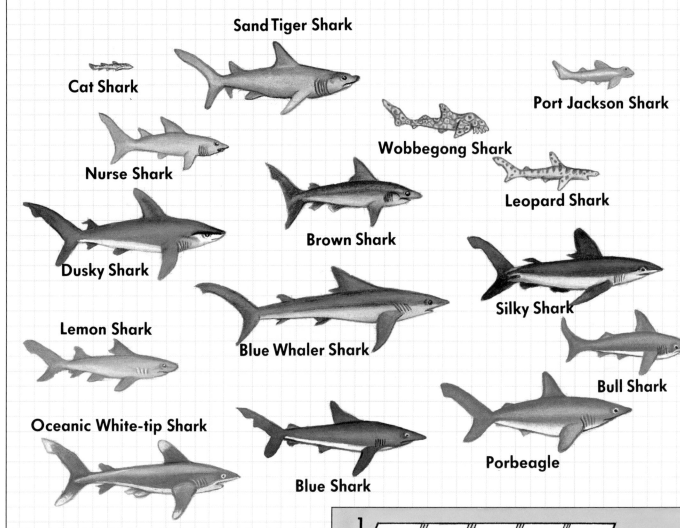

Sand Tiger Shark

Cat Shark

Port Jackson Shark

Wobbegong Shark

Nurse Shark

Leopard Shark

Brown Shark

Dusky Shark

Silky Shark

Lemon Shark

Blue Whaler Shark

Bull Shark

Oceanic White-tip Shark

Porbeagle

Blue Shark

Draw a life-size shark

1. Make yourself a huge sheet of paper.
2. Divide it into (roughly) one-foot (30cm) squares.
3. Copy your shark from these pages, using the squares here to help you.
4. Color in your shark.
5. Cut it out carefully.
6. You can mount it on stiff board.

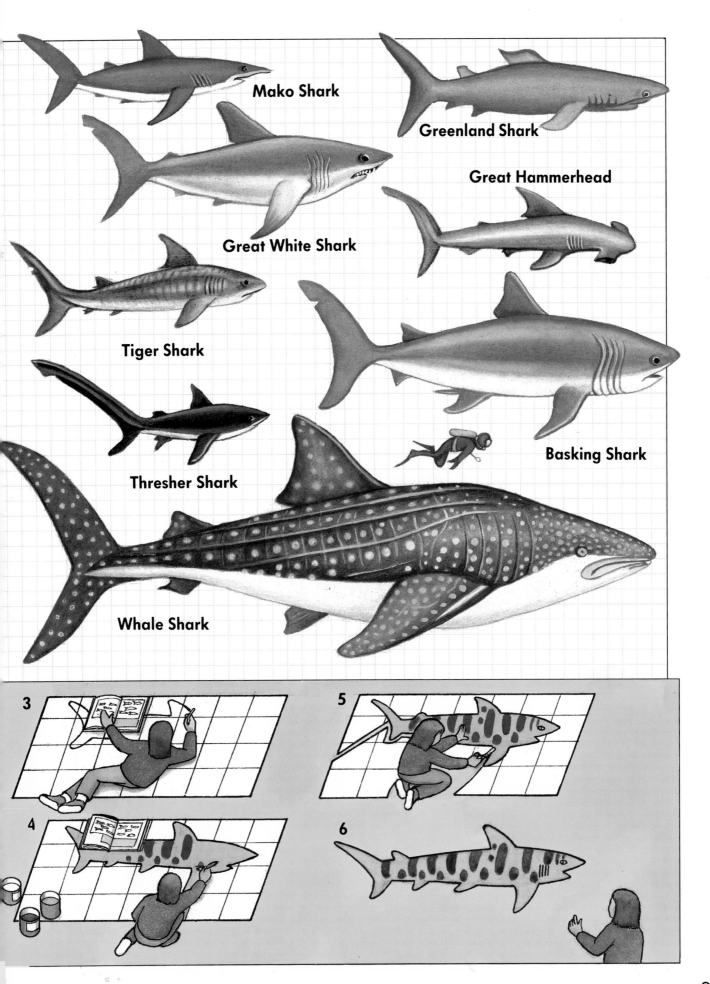

Mako Shark

Greenland Shark

Great Hammerhead

Great White Shark

Tiger Shark

Basking Shark

Thresher Shark

Whale Shark

3

4

5

6

Index

The picture on the cover shows a Great White Shark

Photographic credits: Cover, title page, contents page and pages 9, 16, 18, 19, 25, 30 and 31 (top): Planet Earth; pages 6, 14, 21, 22 and 31 (bottom): Ardea; pages 10 and 26: Zefa; page 13: Frank Lane Agency; page 23: Bruce Coleman.